A celebration of SPRING in rhyme

Mariana Books
Rhyming Series
Book B Seasons

By
Roger Carlson

When the days get longer,
and the cold starts to fade away;
spring is around the corner;
it gets closer with each
passing day.

The nights begin to dwindle,
while the daylight starts shining more;
the weather isn't harsh
or cold like it was before.

Thick white snow,
melts into thin grey slush;
spring takes its time
to unfold; it's not in a rush.

3

The frost gradually thaws,
till there's no chill left in the air;
you see signs of life emerging,
here, there, and everywhere.

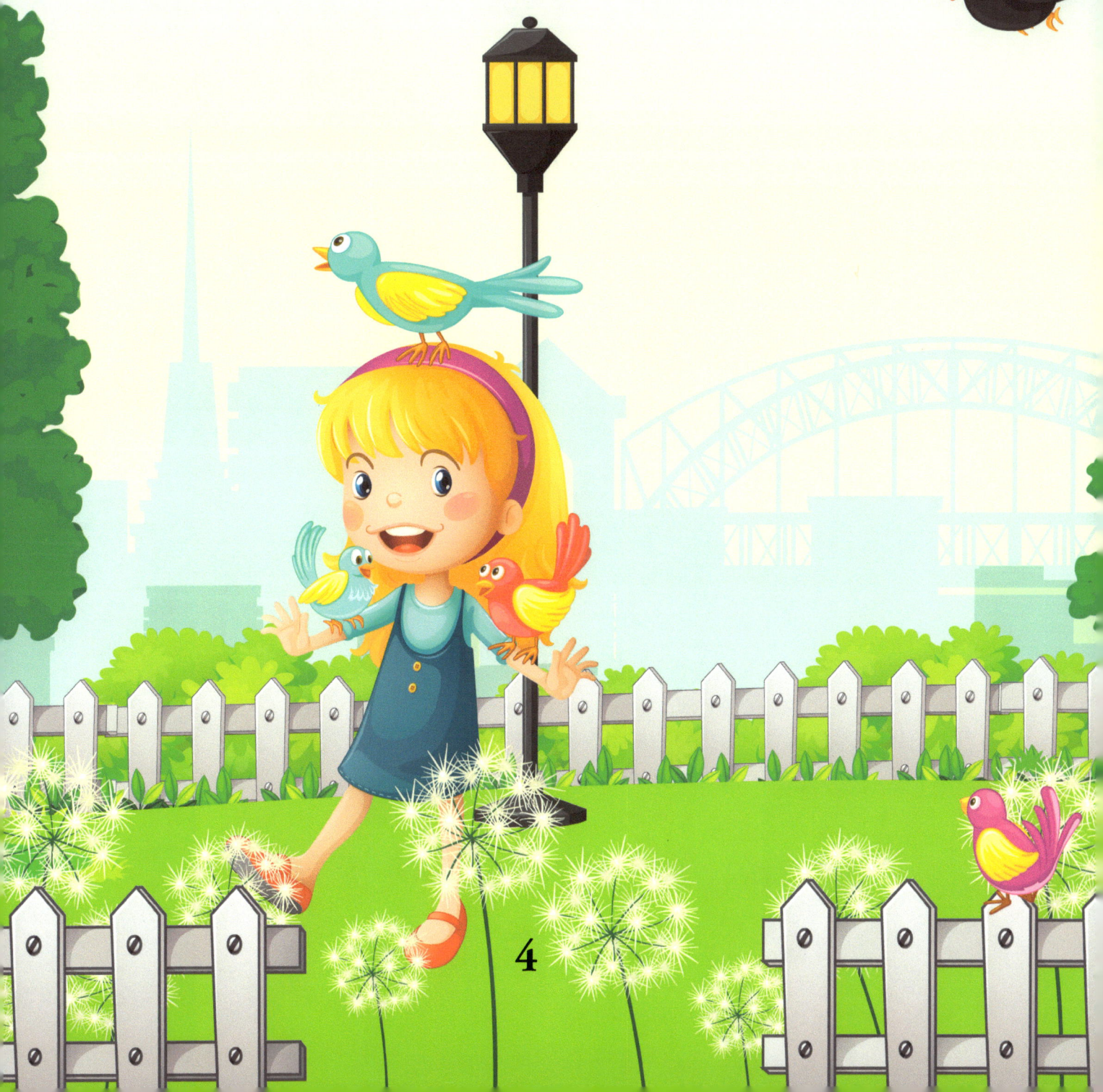

Spring marks the end,
of the cold winter season;
everything starts anew,
and springtime is the reason.

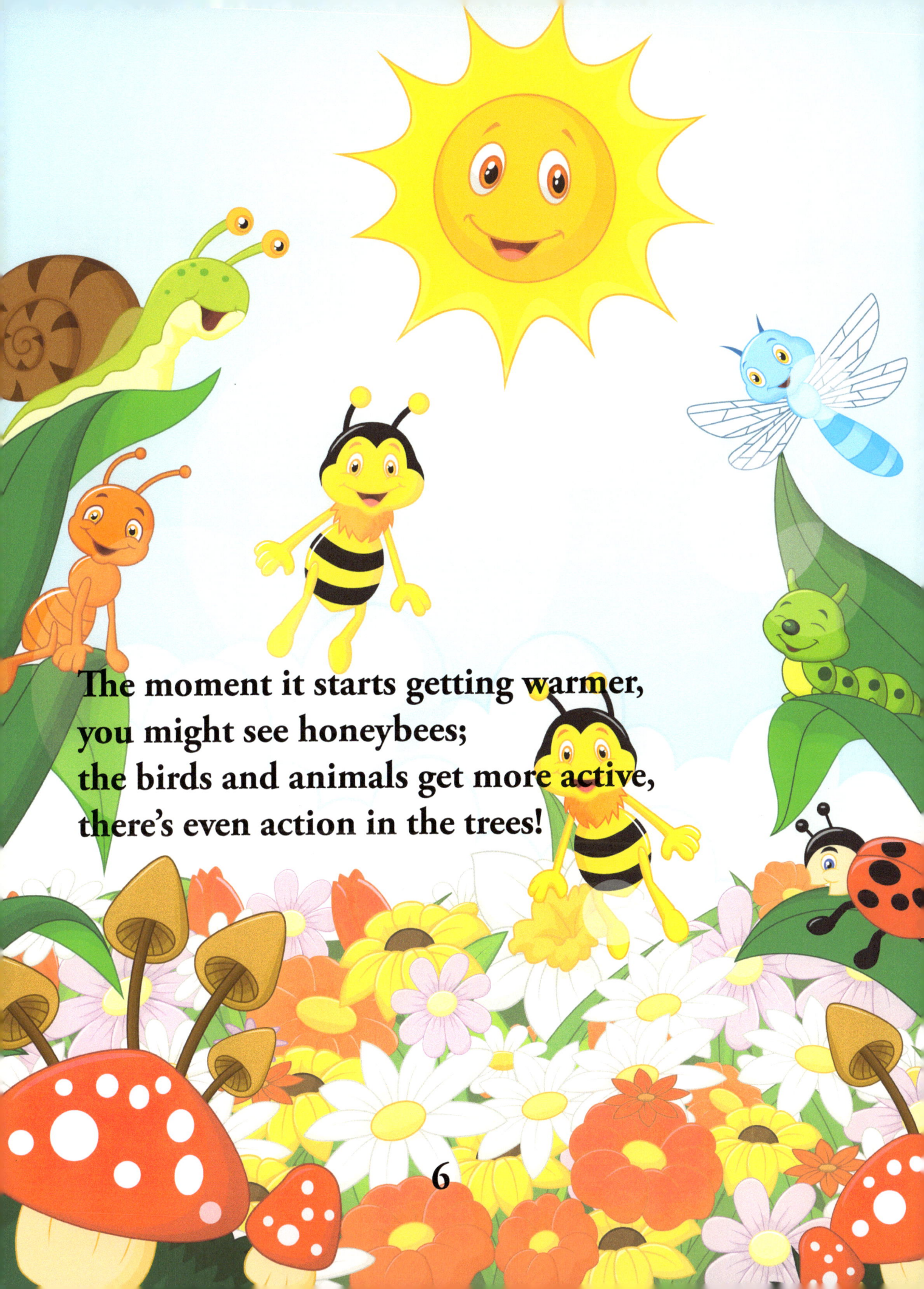

The moment it starts getting warmer,
you might see honeybees;
the birds and animals get more active,
there's even action in the trees!

The trees slowly wake up,
and their leaves start to grow;
they start as buds and open up;
they drink from melting snow.

Everywhere that you look,
you'll see tiny shoots of green;
new plants start sprouting up,
creating a colorful scene.

As spring advances,
more flowers start to bloom;
lilacs, daisies, and daffodils,
fight dandelions for room.

Earthy lilies dance,
with their petals towards the sun;
tulips emerge in all colors,
a different shade for every one!

Take a walk in a meadow,
you'll see a rainbow of tulips before you;
red, yellow, orange, purple,
pink, violet, and bright blue!

But flowers aren't the only ones
that pop up to greet the sun;
lots of vegetables also sprout,
by the time that spring is done.

Farmers scatter seeds,
on the freshly plowed ground;
soon, crops will be aplenty,
growing all around.

How about some asparagus?
It's long, green, and thin.
Or what about black-eyed peas?
Or some kale from this farmer's bin?

In spring, you'll see all kinds of animals emerge from their hiding places; they'll look up towards the sun to feel it warm their faces.

Sleepy brown bears
poke their heads out of caves to see;
red and brown foxes tumble
out of their holes, thick and furry.

Soon, you'll find baby animals
squeaking and squawking away;
bunnies, ducklings, chipmunks,
and baby squirrels to make your day!

The birds that flew south,
start making the journey back;
they're always on time for spring,
and they travel in a pack!

After a hard winter's break,
after lots of winter rest;
birds come back once it's warm,
and start building a new spring nest.

They might come to your window,
a sure sign that spring is here;
you can put some food out,
don't get too close or they'll disappear!

The air is filled with chirps,
and songs sound shrill and sweet;
to hear all the birds sing,
in spring is such a treat!

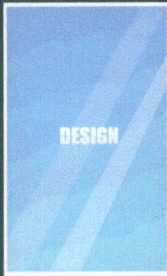

Sunshine and fresh air
stream into every home;
spring is the healthiest season,
no matter where you roam!

DESIGN

Finally, pack the sweaters away,
this really means one thing;
you're ready to go outside,
and enjoy the feeling of spring!

You don't have to wrap yourself
in gloves, scarves, coats, and hats;
throw on your favorite pair of jeans,
a light shirt and that's that!

Run outside, leap over rocks,
jump as high as you can go;
no more freezing feet or chilly breath,
and finally, no more snow!

People go out to parks,
since sunlight will increase;
after a long, harsh winter,
spring brings its own peace.

Here's to the first full season,
of the brand-new year;
a season that's filled with light,
as the days are growing clear.

We hope that your spring,
is so good it can't be beat;
enjoy the nice weather,
before it turns to summer heat!

Find these and all of the other Mariana Publishing books for sale on Amazon and our web site
www.marianapublishing.com

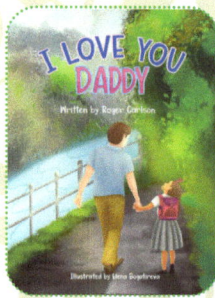

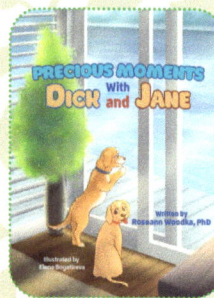

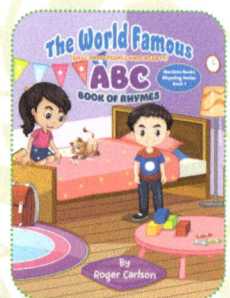

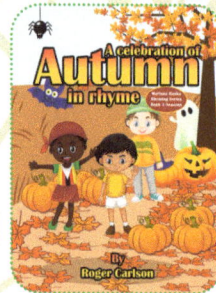

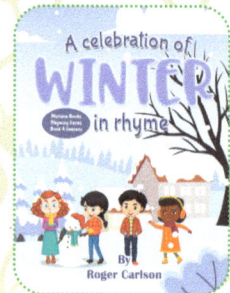

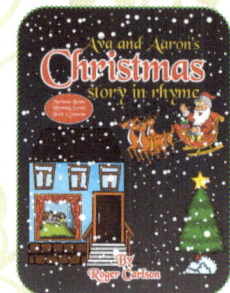

WAYBACK BOOKS

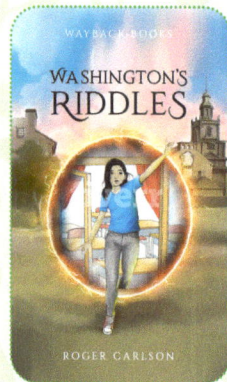

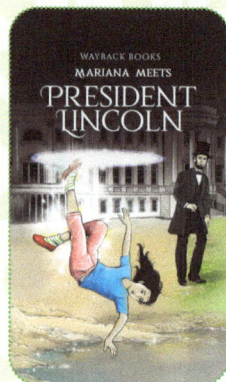

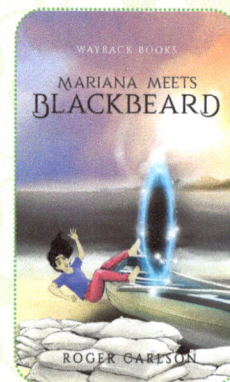

Find us on:

f @marianapublishing   📷 @marianapublishing   🐦 @LlcMariana   ▶ Mariana Publishing Online

Copyright © 2020 by Roger Carlson

ISBN: 978-1-64510-051-5 (Hardback)
ISBN: 978-1-64510-050-8 (Amazon Paperback)
ISBN: 978-1-64510-052-2 (Print On Demand)